What the Heck is a Frame-Pedestal Aesthetic?
1960s Revolution in American Art Revisited

by Alec Clayton

What the Heck is a Frame-Pedestal Aesthetic?
1960s Revolution in American Art Revisited

by Alec Clayton
Originally published as *A Ground for Today's Art:
An Alternative to the Frame-Pedestal Aesthetic*
Cover photo: Teri Bevelacqua working on her billboard at Burning Man. Photo by Benjamin Von Wong.

Copyright © 2020 by Alec Clayton

All rights reserved.

No part of this book may be reprinted or transmitted in any form or by any means, electronic or mechanical, including photocopying, recording, or by any information storage or retrieval system, without permission in writing by the copyright owner.

ISBN: 9798664224030

MFP Mud Flat Press

Dedication and Acknowledgements

Dedicated to Richard C of Carbondale, Illusion, who introduced me to Ray Johnson and the New York Correspondance School (misspelling intentional for reasons that will become clear when you read the book) and who continues to send me mail art to this day.

Thanks to my graduate thesis advisor George Moldovan.

Thanks to our housemate Madeline Morgan who jokingly said we should put "soon to be a major motion picture" on the cover. Maddie Jean, in case you haven't noticed, I have been known to take jokes literally.

Thanks to Jennifer Olson, art historian and Gallery Director at Tacoma Community College, and Becky Hendrick, author of *Getting It: A Guide to Understanding and Appreciating Art*, for reading the manuscript and writing cover blurbs.

And thanks to my wife, Gabi Clayton, who edits almost every word I ever write and helps with cover art and design on all my books, this one included.

Author's Note

This book was written as my graduate thesis in 1970. Only a handful of copies were printed, one for me, one for my graduate thesis advisor, and one for the university library, East Tennessee State University, and possibly one for the Art Department. I don't know if any other copies were printed. It was never published for general consumption, but only printed by the college and bound with a hard cover.

It was my wife, Gabi Clayton, who suggested we should publish it. Upon re-reading it, I agreed with her that it should be published. I now see that the thesis is, in essence, an explanation of what is called Postmodernist art, a term that was just beginning to show up in art journals in the 1970s. I had never heard of Postmodernism in 1970, but I see now that I wrote about it without knowing that was what it was called.

There are a few things in these pages I would not say if I were writing this book today. As a prime example, the use of the masculine generic word *men* or *man* to refer to all humankind. Art histories and articles in popular art journals at the time almost completely ignored both women artists and artists of color. Women and people of color are not mentioned in this text. If I were writing it today, I would be sure to include mention of artists such as Faith Ringgold, Jean-Michel Basquiat and Judy Chicago.

Some of my ideas about art have evolved in the fifty years since I wrote this. I have not "corrected" any of my statements from fifty years ago, but I have let my words stand with only a few minor grammar and spelling corrections that do not change the ideas.

I have added some photographs. Note also that in 1970 I spelled my name Alex not Alec.

A Ground for Today's Art:
An Alternative to the Frame-Pedestal Aesthetic

A Thesis
Presented to
The Faculty of the Graduate School
East Tennessee State University

In Partial Fulfillment
of the Requirements for the Degree
Master of Arts

George Moldovan
Chairman, Advisory Committee

by
John Alexander Clayton
August 1970

Table of Contents

Chapter		Page
I.	Introduction	1
II.	Historical Developments	8
	De Kooning's No-Environment	
	Jackson Pollock	
III	A Look at the Contemporary Scene	24
	New Attitudes	
	I am for an art	
	Andy Warhol	
	Humor	
	Literal art	
	Collage	
IV	Conclusion	37
V	Afterword	50
VI	A Post-Postmodern Postscript	54
VII	Bibliography	56

List of Figures

1. Mail art by Ray Johnson   39
2. Collage by Alex Clayton   40
3. Mail art by Ray Johnson   41
4. Mail art by Richard C   42
5. Mail art by Richard C   43
6. Mail art by Richard C   44
7. New York Correspondence School   45
8. Collage by Alec Clayton   46
9. Mail art by Richard C   47
10. Collage by Alec Clayton   48
11. Mail art by Richard C   49
12. Collage by Ray Johnson, Richard C and Alec Clayton   51

Chapter 1

Introduction

The world in which we live is at this moment seemingly in a state of flux, with an unprecedented upheaval of preconceived notions about religion, art, and philosophy. Governmental and educational systems are being re-evaluated by an increasing number of people, as are areas of culture and patterns of living. These changes can be witnessed to on the one hand by "dropouts," people who are giving up conventional life and family living, quitting their jobs or schools and living in tribal communes, and, on the other hand, by people who have not dropped out of society but are challenging the values of established orders through political and social protest.

    Perhaps most notably, it is through the youth of the world that change is made evident. And vast numbers of today's youth are questioning practically all pre-conceived notions of what is good, what is bad, and what is important. They are, in fact, questioning the very validity of such time-honored dualities as right-wrong and good-bad. As implied by John Cage, "The situation must be yes-and-no not either-or. *Avoid a polar situation.*"[1]

    The art of man is both a manifestation of change and evidence of it. According to Marshall McLuhan, the artist "anticipates the changes in man . . . and through his work adjusts the collective psyche to it."[2] As in nearly every facet

---

[1] John Russell and Suzi Gablik, Pop Art Redefined (New York: Frederick A. Praeger, 1969), p. 23.
[2] Harold Rosenberg, "Understanding Media," McLuhan: Hot and Cool, ed. Gerald E. Stearn (New York: Signet, 1969), p. 198.

of the contemporary society, there seem to be vast changes taking place in the newer art, changes that may defy understanding if approached with an aesthetic posture from another era.

During the Renaissance an aesthetic came into being that gained near universal acceptance in the Western World. With the advantage of hindsight, we can now look back at that aesthetic and the art the grew out of it and derive a fairly definitive idea of what art was at that time. The work of art was an artifact, the product of man's ingenuity and skill, an orderly arrangement of visual elements placed in a frame or on a pedestal, standing as a visual interpretation of the world as men of that time seemed to think it out to be. Once firmly established, this conception of art (which can now be seen as the tradition of easel painting or a frame-pedestal aesthetic) continued almost unquestioned for nearly five hundred years, with the ever-present frame acting as a window through which man can envision the world.

While it is true that there has been talk of a revolution in art beginning with Cubism in the first years of the twentieth century, it appears now that the revolution represented only an alternative in forms. The conception of art as a window on the world was perhaps changed to a conception of the artifact as an object. But there remained the implication that the artist is a special class of person and the work of art a special class of object. Still producing artifacts to be displayed in museums, the Cubists did not seriously infringe upon the continuity of easel painting or pedestal sculpture.

Judging by the nature of works being produced today by an increasing number of artists, the old traditions are no longer relevant to this new data. For these artists, art has ceased to be a look at the world as is, acting "directly on experience, instead of being something that stands for it."[3]

The contemporary world in all its complexity is perhaps best described by McLuhan, whose explorations into the effects of media have "started an uncommon international cultural squabble."[4] Although McLuhan's thesis is perhaps too neatly tied up in one narrow rudiment, it does offer a plausible description of the flux of today's world, especially as it relates to art.

As interpreted by this author, McLuhan's thesis is that environments, as well as patterns of thought and action, are determined by media. This phenomenon results from the particular sensory apparatus involved in perceiving a given media, so that, according to McLuhan, a visual society would be one in which print is the predominant media. McLuhan contends that while the primary media since the Renaissance has been the printed page, it is now being superseded by telegraph, television and radio, o electronic media. Events occur in a print-oriented society in a sequence akin to the orderly arrangement of words in a book. Just as reading is a rather slow and intimate process, one word at a time and left to right, progress since the Renaissance has been relatively slow, with events occurring one at a time in linear pattern. McLuhan speaks of visual space, the world of print technology, as being uniform, continuous and connected, and cites as evidence the art of the Renaissance with its insistence of linear perspective. "The viewer of Renaissance art is systematically placed outside the frame of the experience. A piazza for everything and everything in its piazza."[5]

---

[3] Russell and Gablik, p. 15.
[4] Rosenberg, p. XIII.
[5] Marshall McLuhan and Quentin Fiore, *The Medium is the Message* (New York: Bantam Books, Inc., 1967), unpaginated.

In today's electronic world events no longer occur one at a time in a conveniently linear pattern. Like the images that bombard us from our television screens, history is instantaneous, a collage of events.[6] The contemporary world is no longer primarily visual. It is a world of electronic media which involves all the senses. Time and space are "integrated . . . acoustic, horizonless, boundless, olfactory. . . ."[7]

Analogies may be drawn between the development of art leading up to the twentieth century and the change from print to electronic media a discussed by McLuhan. In sequential, linear order, new schools of art may have followed one another in the neat packaged order that art history texts would have us believe.[8] This seems to have been the case until the early twentieth century, at which time the stable order began to fragment. Concurrent with this fragmentation process, there was a break from the Renaissance aesthetic, both of which may have been first hinted at with the advent of Cubism. Cubism may have destroyed the tyranny of representation and the rule of perspective, through abstraction; it may have scorned the sacredness of oil on canvas by introducing the *papier colle*, but it did not seriously challenge the frame-pedestal aesthetic. After Cubism, the fragmentation seeming redoubled, until at best it can safely be said that the diffusion is collage-like, with many styles and changes occurring simultaneously. Today the list of "isms" is seemingly endless, with such "schools" as Pop, Op, Hard Edge

---

[6] Collage as a media and as a method of design is a factual representation of the world in that there is no arbitrary or idealistic order imposed by the artist. Te opposite of this would be perspective as a method of design and oil paint as a media. Oil paint, which has been a favorite media of art for centuries, is now being replaced with new media by many artists.

[7] McLuhan and Fiore.

[8] Linear order from Baroque and Rococo, through Realism, Impressionism, and so forth.

Abstraction, Minimal, Dirt Art, Happenings, Funk Art, and many more existing concurrently.

Following Cubism, the next jolt to the art public was probably Dada. "Anti-art, antiwar, antimaterialism, and antirationalism,"[9] the Dadaists attempted to overthrow all aesthetics. For all its flamboyance, however, Dada actually overthrew nothing. If the Dadaists failed to destroy tradition, they at least stepped off the pedestal that artists had been on for centuries, and beckoned others to follow suit. In this sense Dada may be seen as a forecast of artists giving up their exalted position increasingly in favor of the more contemporary stance of a man "doing his thing."

Despite the shock of Dada, the linear development of art continued.[10] Many of the outmoded canons of beauty fought desperate but hopeless battles in exhibitions and critical press. At last, in the second quarter of the twentieth century, the tradition of easel painting was seriously challenged by the Abstract Expressionists, who began to form an ethical rather than an aesthetic base for art. Relating to existentialism, they were concerned with freedom and experience, and placed special emphasis on the act of painting.

Following close on the heels of Abstract Expressionism, Allan Kaprow and others devised a form of art (Happenings) that denied all traditions by combining all media and the various senses, by doing away with the spectator and setting up conditions that prevented control on the part of the

---

[9] Barbara Rose, *American Art Since 1900* (New York: Frederick A. Praeger, 1967), p. 96.
[10] As already implied, the linearity of art history is a convenience to the critic that has been gained through retrospect. This author makes no claim that the development of art has taken a linear pattern. Such patterns exist only when imposed by historians and are valid only in so far as they serve to illuminate particular concepts and do not claim to be statements of irrefutable fact.

artist. With the advent of Happenings and Pop Art, and their wide acceptance, the aims of Dada were belatedly achieved.

Since Pop, or using it as a convenient point of demarcation, the currency of naming "new schools" based on stylistic qualities seems evermore in question, Pop itself being a case in point as to the fallibility of the convenience of labels.[11] It follows, therefore, that a point has been reached at which basic assumptions must be reevaluated. For this reason, a number of contemporary artists are developing new ethical-aesthetic criteria.

For the new artist, a concern with aesthetics of any kind, but especially conventional aesthetics, which always implicitly suggests formal stylistic guidelines, is becoming less and less relevant. The work of art is more a manifestation of ethical posture. Such was the case with Pop Art, but the roots of this new concern can be traced back to Abstract Expressionism. As early as 1944, new concerns with art-as-ethic were indicated by Robert Motherwell, who was perhaps unique in that he "valued painting as a source of pleasure, a value it had seldom, if ever, been assigned in America."[12] Motherwell saw "the history of modern art . . . as the history of modern freedom"[13] and said that "in the greatest painting, the painter communes with himself."[14]

The ground of art appears to have moved from aesthetic to ethic-aesthetic to ethics. What is at stake may well

---

[11] When Pop first emerged, many critics tried to apply old ideas of stylistic categorization, only to find that generalizations based on style did not bear up to the facts presented by Pop. In 1969 a new book, appropriately titled *Pop Art Redefined*, approached Pop Art from an ethical rather than an aesthetical standpoint, admitting deficiencies in classification by style. See Russell and Gablik.
[12] Rose, p. 178.
[13] Robert Motherwell, "The Modern Painter's World," as quoted in Rose, p. 178.
[14] Motherwell.

be what an artist does and his awareness of the world situation, not how beautifully the artifact is made. This paper is an exploration into the new ethic and the historic and environmental milieu from which it has emerged. Through this, it is hoped that an understanding of a reasonable ground for a new art shall be set.

Chapter II
Historical Developments

Irreverent commentary in the form of Marcel Duchamp's painting of 1918, titled "T'um" may be an early example of a desire on the part of some artists to find an alternative to the traditional aesthetics that still remained after Cubism. In this painting, Duchamp "recapitulated the plastic vocabulary of the painter to that date,"[15] incorporating into its examples of the predominant visual devices of art to that date (perspective, illusion and *trompe l'oeil*), as well as concrete examples of important particulars in his own bag of tricks. To Duchamp this may or may not have been a comic gesture, but in retrospect it appears hilarious, as do the similar but more recent "Erased de Kooning" and the companion pieces "Factum I" and "Factum II" by Robert Rauschenberg, and Roy Lichtenstein's "Little Big Painting." The "Erased de Kooning" is precisely what the title indicates, a de Kooning drawing that Rauschenberg erased, thus making another drawing of it—his own. "Factum I" is a typical action painting, complete with drips and splashes of color that seemingly could never be repeated, a very personal statement. "Factum II" is its identical twin. The Lichtenstein is a single brush stroke, a stylized picture of a

---

[15] Christopher Finch, Pop Art: Object and Image (New York: Dutton and Co., Inc., 1968), p. 19.

splash of color, perhaps de Kooning's, executed in a slick, commercial manner. These paintings by Rauschenberg and Lichtenstein seem to dismiss summarily the esoteric style of action painting, a style to which both were much indebted. Doing much the same thing, the effect of Duchamp's "T'um" was perhaps much stronger for a least three reasons: First, the time. In 1918 there were no historical precedents in the fine arts for this kind of comic gesture. Second, the pictorial devices Duchamp dismissed were, for the most part, of his own invention. And third, it was allegedly his last painting. In giving up painting in the limited sense of easel painting, Duchamp accepted the larger role of an artist as a creative person who is not limited to work in any given media or style.

Two years before Duchamp's "T'um," a German conscientious objector, Hugo Ball, and his countryman poet, Richard Huelsenbeck, opened a Franco-German dictionary at random and picked the first word to meet their eyes: Dada. "And Dada became the name of a movement in the process of birth."[16]

Dada was born of a war that, in the minds of many artists and intellectuals, killed once and for all the idealism of the preceding century, and it grew out of the new artistic freedom given form by Cubism; not unlike the way the new art of today has grown out of Vietnam, student revolt and sexual liberation, as well as visual traditions that in many cases were extensions of Cubism. Dada was not so much anti-art as it was anti-tradition and not so much art as a way of life. Analogies between the Dadaist milieu and today's revolution of youth can be seen in this statement by Barbara Rose:

> Obviously, if the public chose to take modern art as a scandal, the answer was to give them more scandals, unconventional behavior, sexual liberation, even dissipation

---

[16] Marcel Jean, The History of Surrealist Painting, trans. Simon Watson Taylor (New York: Grove Press, 1960), p. 65.

were condoned; chess playing and transvestitism took their place as artistic activities . . .

To the critics that cried out that modern art was immoral and anarchistic, the Dadaists answered in the affirmative, and claimed that the rights of the artist transcended morality and politics.[17]

For the young artist of today, Marcel Duchamp is certainly the grand hero of Dada:

> Aside from being the proto-Dada Duchamp has also been in many ways the anti-Dada par excellence. While the Dadas[sic] exhorted their audience to "stop thinking!" and cried "Bas les mots!" and "Merde a là beaute!" Duchamp was doing nothing but thinking, using words, and even creating new areas of beauty. . . . What better combination than the hero who is dead serious about not being serious?[18]

This picture of Duchamp paints him as the perfect hero for the 1970s. A good example of Duchamp's "proto-Dada, anti-Dada" status can be found in his Fountain and in the letter that Duchamp wrote in defense of it:

The Richard Mutt Case

> They say any artist paying six dollars may exhibit.
> Mr. Mutt [the name Duchamp signed, actually the name of a manufacturer of sanitary hardware] sent in a

---

[17] Rose, p. 97-98.
[18] Lucy Lippard, "New York Letter 1965: Reinhardt, Duchamp, Morris," *The New Art*, ed. Gregory Battcock (New York: E.P. Dutton and Co., Inc., 1966), p. 193.

fountain. Without discussion this article disappears and never was exhibited.

What were the grounds for refusing Mr. Mutt's fountain:
1. Some contended it was immoral, vulgar.
2. Others, it was plagiarism, a plain piece of plumbing.

Now Mr. Mutt's fountain is not immoral, that is absurd, no more than a bathtub is immoral. It is a fixture that you see every day in plumber's show windows.

Whether Mr. Mutt with his own hands made the fountain or not has no importance. He CHOSE it, he took an ordinary article of life, placed it so that its significance disappeared under the new title and point of view—created a new thought for that object.

As for plumbing, that is absurd. The only works of art America has given are her plumbing and her bridges.[19]

Although Duchamp and others survived Dada, the movement itself was short lived. The concepts behind Dada, like any concept or interpretation of what art out to be, can be assaulted, done in to a point that it is no longer a viable force. The Dadaists went to great lengths to deny logic a place in art, and some of their adherents tried to destroy art itself. In so doing, the movement ate itself up.

Many of the artists, as well as the forms of Dada, were assimilated into Surrealism. This evolving of one school into another seems to hold little relevance for today's young artist, to whom there seems to be no chronology. Historical time-place depends on how close to the front of the back of a book a particular event is described, on which book is read first, and upon a hierarchy of events dependent

---

[19] Reprinted from *The Blind Man*, 1917, in Jean, p. 36.

not upon chronological order but upon relevance to personal interest. The way in which Surrealism appeared and its relation to Dada is negligible in the present context. What is important is the rudiment upon which it was developed, automatism, a system whereby the artist gives vent to the subconscious, often by inducing hallucinations or dreamlike states.

The basic assumptions behind automatism have been aptly explained by Marcel Jean:

> The subjective psyche and individual sensation remain inseparable from reality, for they are its living heart and creative brain. To rediscover original sensations and images beneath appearances conventionalized and fixed by habit, to deepen those appearances and give concrete form to hidden realities is the particular role assigned to those whose sight has become second sight. Such people, artists, inventors, poets, see what is in the process of being born . . .
>
> It may be possible to agree with Apollinaire in his dictum that "everyone is a poet," at least theoretically, in in actual fact most people's perception is not adapted to any process of inquiring outside conventional truth. The creative gift, rarely used, remains in a latent state, falling asleep after childhood and most often only showing signs of life in what are called the unconscious forms of the psychic structure: the dream, for instance. It is understandable then, that the new poets and painters [Surrealists] should have wished to study and utilize those mental states in which the visionary faculty seemed to express itself most vigorously: even, where necessary, fomenting such states by appropriate means.[20]

Even if the rhetoric and some of the ideas expressed by Marcel Jean seem romantic and dated, the basic assumption of the importance of the unconscious is still, and always has been, valid. Today's poet

---

[20] Jean, p. 117.

or painter may induce a hallucinatory state through the use of mind-expanding drugs or he may simply have faith in whims. The romantic poets relied on passion recalled.[21] Basically, it is all the same thing, a realization that submerged under the everyday poppycock of cliché and euphemism are memories, perceptions and ideas of consequence. The Surrealists systemized this basic assumption and gave the world concrete evidence of its validity.

As a major movement in art, Surrealism never really held sway in America, but it did serve as an influencing agent, never standing in the spotlight but pushing American art onto center stage. As Sam Hunter put it:

> Of all the artistic influences in the air, the belated discovery of Surrealism was perhaps the most important [in the development of modern American art]. ... The importance of both Dada and Surrealism arose as much from their mood or romantic protest . . . as it did from their actual program or artistic devices.[22]

Taking their cue from Surrealism and employing the formal inventions of Cubism, a group of artists, based mostly in New York, developed a school of art that was to be a dominant force in the West for close to twenty years; finally to be destroyed by its own success. This school was, of course, Abstract Expressionism. Indicative of the preceding statement, and an entertaining summation of the rise and fall of Abstract Expressionism, is the following statement from an interview with Robert Indiana:

Will Pop bury Abstract-Expressionism?

---

[21] William Wordsworth, "Preface to Second Edition of Lyrical Ballads," *The Creative Process*, ed. Brewser Ghiselin (New York: Mentor, 1952), p. 84.
[22] Sam Hunter, Modern American Painting and Sculpture (New York: Dell Publishing Co., Inc., 1959), pp. 133-34.

No. If A-E dies, the abstractionist will bury themselves under the weight of their own success and acceptance; they are battlers and the battle is won; . . . they seem by nature to be teachers and inseminators and their students and followers are legion around the world; they are inundated by their own fecundity. They need birth control.

Will Pop replace Abstract-Expressionism?

In the eternal what-is-new-in-American-painting-shows, yes; in the latest acquisition of the avant-garde collectors, yes; in the American Home, no.[23]

Among numerous Abstract Expressionists who may have played an important role in forging the ground for a new art, Jackson Pollock and Willem de Kooning seem to stand out. Developing their art in the atmosphere of Abstract expressionism, Pollock and de Kooning introduced new concepts that may have proven much more important to the future of art than did the movement itself. They introduced elements that may have signaled the end of the tradition of easel painting. And at the same time when subject matter was taboo for the serious painter, they reintroduced the figure and prophesied pop iconography. In so doing, they began what may be seen as a trend towards the decategorization of art.

As two of the foremost Abstract Expressionists, neither Pollock nor de Kooning felt any compunction about doing things that were not strictly within the limits of their own style.[24] Their work was

---

[23] Gene Swenson, "What is Pop Art?" reprinted in Russell and Gablik, p. 80.

[24] There seems to be a tendency among a number of artists to become enslaved by style. This tendency was described by Picasso in the following way:

When we invented Cubism . . . nobody drew up a program of action. . . . The young painters of today often outline a program for themselves to follow and try to do their assignments correctly like well-behaved school-boys. (Christian Zervos "Conversations with Picasso" *The Creative Process*, pp. 58-59). This tendency to follow a program has been noticed in the work of graduate students

an immediate reaction to their environment, and therefore, the art of these two pointed towards the next generation's emphasis on relating art to life.

To amplify the preceding statements, Jackson Pollock and Willem de Kooning shall be considered individually.

---

in university art departments as well as among practicing artists. As shall be indicated in later chapters, this tendency seems to be increasingly losing force.

De Kooning's No-Environment

In the late forties and fifties, it seemed that no style other than Abstract Expressionism was worthy of the serious painter. This state of affairs may have been due to a somewhat evangelistic posture on the part of the Abstract expressionists, as well as a practical matter of getting accepted by the fashionable galleries. To a large extent, commercial success seemed to be based on a priori assumption that a painting must be loaded with "guts and action," strong emotion, harsh colors, and contain no subject matter. In the face of this prevailing attitude, de Kooning painted women. Not only did he paint women, he painted them pink, that hearts-and-flowers, sickly-sweet, Easter parade of color. Of course de Kooning's women are almost legendary now, and it is commonly accepted that there was never anything "Easter-parady" bout them (perhaps Easter parody).

De Kooning's free interpretation of Cubist space is reminiscent of his one-time studio mate, Arshile Gorky, but while Gorky and other innovators of Abstract Expressionism were very much indebted to Surrealism, de Kooning had no such interest.

His subjects were not the remote evocations of poetic fantasy, but the most tangible realities of the human figure and the urban environment. This preoccupation with the tangible and immediate experiences characterizes de Kooning's tougher, more brutal sensibility.[25]

De Kooning's paintings can be seen as concrete evidence of what a sensitive person may feel when plunging into his environment. And this environment was not, and is not, void of subject matter. Rather, it is one of strangulation masses of people, an environment that demands involvement. To put this idea in terms of McLuhan's media-controlled world: "One of the consequences of electronic environments is the total involvement of people in people."[26]

Although de Kooning's primary concern seems to have been with the act of painting and the language of art, he has used his art to comment on his time, referring to the ambiguous space of his paintings as the "No-environment, a metaphor for the dislocated space in which the flux of modern life takes place."[27] His particular no-environment was New York City, television, movies, billboards, blatant commercialism and plastic sexuality, a complete lack of privacy and a constant variety: a collage of life. A de Kooning could never have existed in a small Southern town or mid-Western village in 1950. In 1970 it is conceivable that he could exist in almost any locale, no matter how remote.

For de Kooning, the painting was not a gilded monument intended for idle, detached reverence; it was an arena. He seldom dabbled or stroked the canvas; he attacked! And the painting fought back. The painting was life, never complete, but constantly in a state of flux. In the habit of cutting up his drawings and sticking them back together with the parts slightly askew, he often incorporated bits and pieces of his drawings, as well as pieces of newspapers, into his paintings. Ostensibly these elements from the everyday world were not used as subject matter. They simply added another dimension to

---

[25] Rose, p. 182.
[26] Stearn, p. 216.
[27] Rose, p. 184.

the painting, a textural area, a point of contrast, and a break in the unity of the surface. These collaged images serve as a formal element with no calculated reference beyond the painting itself. Yet, it would be gauche to ignore the role of the newspaper or the commercial images that he sometimes used. The newspaper and the smile off the camel pack that de Kooning collaged onto one of his women are other blatant pieces of mass culture. They are easily available, impermanent, cheap, and beneath the dignity of traditionally expected art. In painting Marilyn Monroe, de Kooning must have realized that to many people, she, like the newspaper, was a commodity: blatant, easily available and impermanent.

Jackson Pollock

Jackson Pollock has been the subject of very much critical comment. His unorthodox method, his flamboyant lifestyle and tragic death make for interesting press. In surveying some of the myriad articles about Pollock, a number of somewhat typical statements tend to become noticeable. For example:

> [Pollock] . . . stood amongst the pools of paint he had just poured while others were being formed as he moved about.[28]
>
> Pollock's ambition carried him far beyond the traditional unity of easel painting in search of a more monumental space and a total pictorial experience . . . he painted by standing over a painting and letting paint drip on it from above. . . .
>
> Pollock's predominantly silver monoliths took painting even closer to a kind of fragile, open-form continuous space-sculpture . . . [and] approached solid relief texture . . .

---

[28] Allan Kaprow, Assemblage, Environments and Happenings (New York: Harry N. Abrams, Inc., 1966), p. 165.

[and he let] his pigment clot . . . by slapping the unsized edges of the canvas with his paint-dripped palms.[29]

He later also established his connection with Dada's mood of iconoclasm and disgust with society first by his violent imagery and then by his non-esthetic industrial textures, and by embedding cigarette ends, broken glass and bits of string in his pigment.[30]

Statements by Hunter and one by Kaprow were chosen as being typical of a wealth of rhetoric which suggests that Pollock's art represents a battle against an unknown enemy, a presence that he perhaps felt but could not define. Since the motives of a deceased person can only be guessed at and reassessed in view of current data, it is only conjecture that the battles Pollock fought were waged against the confines of an aesthetic that he felt to be outmoded, the tradition of easel painting.[31]

Kaprow suggested that the confines of this tradition have at last been broken by artists, who taking their cue from Pollock, have invented forms such as Environments and Happenings which have effaced all pre-existing boundaries. Pollock hinted at these new forms by working on the floor on unsized, unstretched canvas, by enlarging his scale, by physically getting into his work (standing on it as he worked), and by using foreign elements in his pigment. While the size of his paintings and the fact that they were not built to last suggest that Pollock was not part of a museum-oriented aesthetic, the fact that his work is in museums, and was during his lifetime, indicates that he subscribed, in part, to the old aesthetic.

One can do no more than speculate as to how far Pollock may have gone in the direction of an environmental art had he not been

---

[29] Hunter, pp. 144-45.
[30] Hunter, p. 147.
[31] See p. 2.

killed in the prime of his artistic maturity. Speaking of Pollock, Kaprow said that he "left us at a point where we must be dazzled by the space and objects of our everyday life."[32] He continued:

> Not satisfied with the suggestion through paint of our senses, we shall utilize the specific substances of sight, sound, movement, people, odors, touch. . . .
> The young artist of today need no longer say "I am a painter. . . . He is simply an "artist." All of life will be open to him.[33]

This prophecy of Kaprow's was written in 1958 and was a forecast for the sixties. Now that the sixties are history, it can be seen that in many ways his prophecy has been more than fulfilled.

In a series of lectures beginning with those he gave as an instructor at Black Mountain College in 1952 . . . John Cage, like the Surrealists before him, called on artists to efface the boundary between art and life. . . . He attacked preconceived notions about the function, meaning and context of art. He asked such questions as, "Is a truck in a music school more musical that a truck passing by in a street?"[34]

Cage's lectures set a number of young artists off on a journey that had only been hinted at by Pollock and de Kooning. A number of these artists, notably Jim Dine, Claes Oldenburg, Red Grooms and Kaprow, developed a new kind of free-form theater called Happenings.[35] Being events that combined elements from all the arts, Happenings are neither painting, sculpture, theater, music, poetry or

---

[32] Allan Kaprow, "The Legacy of Jackson Pollock," *Art News* (October 1958), p. 24.
[33] Kaprow, *Art News*.
[34] Rose, p. 216.
[35] Allan Solomon, "The New Art," Battcock, pp. 77-78.

dance. They are simply art. Like the contemporary world as described by McLuhan, Happenings are acoustic, horizonless, boundless, olfactory, a collage of sights, sounds, movement, touch and smells. They do not hang in museums; once they are done they no longer exist, and in many instances there is no audience. And finally, there is very little, if any, manipulation on the part of the artist.[36]

After developing their artistic sensibilities in the milieu of Environments and Happenings, Dine and Oldenburg gained fame as practitioners of Pop Art, a new art that won popular acclaim in the sixties. Pop is an art that has perhaps mistakenly been referred to as a "school" or "style." According to Gablik, the fundamental notions from which both Happenings and Pop emerged was the notion that art must have a "manifest connection with the environment; it must act directly on experience, instead of being something that stands for it."[37] She goes on in the same statement to say that these two forms are closely related and that they continue to co-exist.[38] In this sense, the apparent "apartness" of Happenings and Pop, as discussed by art historians, may represent nothing more realistic than a convenience in outlining their discussions. Pop, therefore, may be thought of as the concepts of Happenings expressed in forms taken from easel painting.[39]

The images of Pop are banal images borrowed from mass culture, from movies, television, comic books and advertising. More often than not, they are found images that exist in a two-dimensional form a priori, thus reducing the role of the artist as manipulator and increasing the reliance on chance. This use of found imagery

---

[36] Kaprow, *Assemblage, Environments and Happenings*, pp. 188-202.
[37] Russell and Gablik, p. 15, see also p. 2, 3, this paper.
[38] Russell and Gablik.
[39] The use of paint and canvas and numerous examples of Pop Art in museums is an undeniable connection with easel painting traditions, and formal devise of design and color usable that may be traced to conventional aesthetics do exist. These things may be usable tools rather than aspects of a tradition as a limiting agent.

presented at face value with little or no manipulation or comment by the artist represents an ethic, or moral strategy, not unlike that of Pollock or Kaprow.[40] What the artist choses to do becomes more critical than how well he does it.

In the short time that it took Pop to win critical acclaim, a number of its adherents were already moving into new areas of exploration. Simultaneously, some continued to work in Happenings, Environments and related fields.[41] Andy Warhol is making movies. Oldenburg plans monuments that may be thought of as purely conceptual art, in that hey either cannot be built or are not expected to be built. Larry Rivers has made something that he calls sculpture, which consists of models wearing fashions of his design; while Tom Wesselmann has found a new twist for his *Great American Nude* and *Still Life*, building three-dimensional still life structures in a box, complete with cutout holes through which a hidden model protrudes her nude breasts.

The apparent conclusion is that these artists, among others, give proof to Kaprow's statement that all of life will be open to the new artist.[42]

---

[40] Russell and Gablik, pp. 17-18.
[41] Environments and Happenings have been mentioned in conjunction, Environments being the form out of which Happenings grew; see Kaprow, p.184.
[42] See p. 24.

Chapter III

A Look at the Contemporary Scene

A person in search of art today may possibly be confronted with anything from dirt to brainwaves, to an exhibition of words. He may find an exhibition in the streets or in a loft; there may be music, dancing, or even a wrestling match. The domain of painting and sculpture, it seems, has been taken over by poets, television comedy writers, farmers and actors. What seems to be happening is that an increasing number of artists, who date back to the late forties and who gained momentum with Pop Art, are approaching their work with new attitudes that seem to be direct manifestations of the contemporary society; giving up old ideas of style in favor of a concern with content and moving freely between different styles and different media.

    Out of this kaleidoscope of artistic activity, a few characteristic features began to appear. Given the present lack of hindsight and the volatile nature of much of art, little can be done by way of generalization or explanation. One can, however, take a long look at what is going on, in an attempt to become sensitive to things as they happen. To sensitize myself I have isolated certain characteristics of today's art that seem to be the most predominant at this time.[43]

1. New attitudes that implicitly exclude conventional aesthetics.
2. An increasing use of humor.
3. An insistence of content over form.
4. The use of collage as media and method.

New Attitudes

The attitudes or ethical posture of an artist must at all times be a personal matter; yet, given environmental and historical conditions which are shared by all artists, common attitudes that allow for individual differences should be a possibility. With a wealth of critical and historical literature and means of easy communication, today's artist can form his own attitudes by studying those of other artists in view of his own situation; therefore, an ethical posture has grown out of that of the recent past, modified to fit present conditions.

Motherwell's idea of art as a source of pleasure seems to be very much in evidence today, perhaps t a much greater degree.[44] Other attitudes, man of which can be traced to John Cage, have lasted and seem to be gaining wider acceptance. Cage's "delight in the accidental and unpredictable, and his total avoidance of qualitative judgments,"[45] gained such popularity that it became a standard for a number of Pop Artists. As explained by Gablik:

---

[43] The terms "today's art" and "the new art: as used from this point throughout refer to ongoing concerns among contemporary artists, as indicated throughout this paper. Such generalizations as may be made about today's art are not intended to be true of *all* art being produced at this time.
[44] See p. 9.
[45] Solomon, p. 77.

> ... [using] chance techniques or "found" rather than invented images, represents in America what really amounts to a moral strategy. . . . By moral strategy I mean any means used to achieve a tougher art, to avoid tasteful choices, and to set the stakes higher.[46]

As with a commitment to chance, age's critical detachment has also gained currency with a number of today's artists. While perhaps taking Cage's avoidance of judgment as a point of departure, many artists continue to evaluate critically their art and their environment, seeing involvement and detachment as not necessarily contradictory. The implied contradiction is perhaps more apparent than real. This may be seen in statements taken from an interview with Roy Lichtenstein, in which he indicates a use of detachment:

> *Is Pop Art Despicable?*
> ... it is an involvement with what I think to be the most brazen and threatening characteristics of our culture, things we hate, but which are also powerful in their impingement on us. ... Pop Art looks out into the world; it appears to accept its environment, which is not good or bad, but different—another state of mind.[47]

Throughout the interview, Lichtenstein doubled back further to elaborate the same concerns:

> ... There are certain things that are usable, forceful and vital about commercial art. We're using those things—but we're not really advocating stupidity, international teenagerism and terrorism.

---

[46] Russell and Gablik, p. 18, see also p. 27, this paper.
[47] Swenson, "What is Pop Art?" Russell and Gablik, p. 92.

> The heroes depicted in comic books are fascist types, but I don't take them seriously in these paintings—maybe there is a point in not taking them seriously, a political point. I use them for purely formal reasons, and that's not what those heroes were invented for. . . .[48]

One artist, Andy Warhol, may be seen as the epitome of new artistic attitudes, and another, Oldenburg, has written an essay that describes his attitudes in a most entertaining manner. To elaborate further the present concerns, Warhol and Oldenburg's essay shall be approached individually.

I Am for an Art

The following is quoted in part from Oldenburg's *Store Days*:

> I am for an art that is political-erotical-mystical, that does something other than sit on its ass in a museum.
> I am for an art that imitates the human, that is comic, if necessary, or violent, or whatever is necessary.
> I am for an art that takes its form from the lines of life itself, that twists and extends and accumulates and spits and drips, and is heavy and coarse and blunt and sweet and stupid as life itself.
> I am for an artist who vanishes, turning up in a white cap painting signs or hallways.
> I am for art under the skirts, and the art of pinching cockroaches.
> I am for the art of conversation between the sidewalk and a blind man's metal stick.

---

[48] Swenson, pp. 92-93.

> I am for U.S. Government Inspected Art, Grade A art, Regular Price art, Yellow Ripe art, Extra Fancy art, Ready-to-eat art, Best-for-less art, Ready-to-cook art, Fully cleaned art, Spend Less art, Eat Better art, Ham art, pork art, chicken art, cake art, cookie art.[49]
>
> Andy Warhol

An observation of the vast array of things Warhol has done in a relatively short period of time indicates that what he is presenting to the public is not so much a collection of art treasures, as it is an approach to life, a lifestyle that is geared to the here and now, constantly open for change. While enjoying tremendous commercial success, in 1965, Warhol announced: "I'm a retired artist."[50] And in the five years since, he has made movies, television commercials, written a book, and pioneered "psychedelic mixed media entertainment."[51]

Mysterious, comical, philosophical, and constantly seeking attention, everything that he does seems to be stamped with a unique "Warholian" flair. For example, he once sent an actor on a college lecture tour. When the hoax was discovered, Warhol explained that the actor was "more like what people expect Andy Warhol to be than he himself could possibly be."[52]

This same kind of passive attitude is noticeable in some of Warhol's well-known aphorisms:

> I like boring things.
> I want to be a machine.

---

[49] Oldenburg, in Russell and Gablik, pp. 97-99.
[50] Paul Carroll, "What's a Warhol?" *Playboy*, XVI (September, 1969), p. 134.
[51] Carroll.
[52] Carroll.

> In the future everybody will be world famous for 15 minutes.[53]
>
> I want everybody to think alike.
>
> I think it would be so great if more people took up silk screens so that no one would know whether my picture was mine or somebody else's.[54]

One may ask why any intelligent person would let somebody else speak for him or want his work to be indistinguishable from another person's work. The probable answer is that (1) Warhol does not think of the work of art as a special class of object, and (2) people are going to hear what they want to hear, no matter what is said. Aware of this, Warhol is apparently content to give the public what it wants. For instance, in a recent issue of *Esquire*, Warhol is pictured surrounded by the material for an upcoming exhibit:

> People (mostly his friends) whom he will exhibit and then rent out. . . . "People only want art so they can talk about it," says Warhol. "This way they can take the art home, have a party for it, show it to their friends, take Polaroids of it (which I will sign), make tape recordings. And after the week is over they'll still have anecdotes."[55]

Humor

> Humor as a system of communication and as a probe of our environment . . . affords us out most appealing anti-establishment tool. It does not deal in theory, but in immediate

---

[53] Carroll.
[54] Swenson, pp. 116-117.
[55] "Work in Progress," *Esquire*, ed. Harold T.P. Hayes, LXXIV (December, 1969), p. 212.

experience, and is often the best guide to changing perceptions.[56]

Quite obviously, if the word art were substituted for the word *art* were substituted for the word *humor*, not only would the preceding quote still make sense, it would sound almost like a paraphrase of Rose of Gablik, an indication that the roles of art and humor in the contemporary world may be essentially the same.[57]

In both the "high" and "low" areas of culture, a new brand of humor seems to be gaining currency. Called "youth humor" in an article by J. Marks, the new humor is bright, fresh and unorthodox.[58] Marks suggests that the kind of prepared jokes with a structured story line leading to a punch line, which were popular a few years ago, are not amusing to today's youth.[59] "Today's humor . . . has no story line."[60] While citing evidence of the same kind of sensibility among some older people, and dating back a number of years, Marks maintains that it is predominantly with today's youth that the new humor exists. Marks further differentiates young people's humor from that of their parents by the casual use of smut, by what he calls "stoned humor" and by the put on.

To many young people taboos on sex, nudity and profanity seem absurd, whereas the real obscenities are words like *war*, *kill*, *nigger*, *Jew*, *cheat* and *lie*. The use of smut that appears in much of their humor is but one way of commenting on what an increasing number of young people apparently see as a false morality:

> There's a lot of smut, it's intentional and it's central to the whole sensibility. Rather than chide the society which sets

---

[56] McLuhan and Fiore.
[57] See pp. 8, 30.
[58] J. Marks, "The New Humor," Esquire, LXXIV (December, 1969), 218.
[59] Marks, 218.
[60] McLuhan and Fiore.

up absurd prohibitions, kids tend to use gross exaggeration and bawdiness as a form of comic comment.[61]

Of course the dirty joke is nothing new, but the old-style dirty joke often seemed to imply that sex was something naughty. To the younger generation, sex may not be dirty, but what has been called "dirty talk" or "smut," is fun, ". . . because it is so harmlessly grotesque when all the insinuation and self-consciousness is removed."[62]

The other two characteristics of youth humor according to Marks, stoned humor and the put on, are very closely related. Take these lines from Good-bye Columbus, for example: "What did you do with yourself this summer? I was growing a penis."[63] That is a smutty put on, and at the same time, it is stoned humor. Although he spoke at length about stones humor, Marks did not offer a neatly packaged definition. Perhaps stoned humor defies definition; it must be experienced. Primarily it is the humor of drug experiences, hash, acid and pot. And it involves the easy bending of time and space and the acceptance of "unheard of levels of abstraction.[64]

The put on, at its most basic, is nothing more than what an earlier generation meant by saying, "you're pulling my leg." But to young people who use it with such apparent ease, it is much more involved, more subtle, and at the same time, more blatant. In many cases a put on is both a joke (a lie) and a truth at the same time, or an exaggerated absurdity presented as truth. Marks said that the put on is based on an assumption that "the entire society is founded on lies and

---

[61] Marks, 220.
[62] Marks, 219.
[63] Marks, 219.
[64] Marks, 330.

therefore small truths are ridiculous because they are only cover for big lies.[65]

The put on can be a handy weapon for celebrities who are often asked rather inane questions by interviewers. Surely everyone is familiar with such questions, things like "what is your favorite color?" As a response to such questions, the Beatles "almost singlehandedly invented the genre."[66]

Question: How tall are you?
Answer: Two feet, nine inches.
Question: What do you do when you're cooped up in a hotel between shows?
Answer: We ice skate.[67]

Literal Art

Much of the newer art may be termed "literal art," in that the content, or what the painting is about, is stated quite explicitly and seems to take precedence over formal considerations. For example, "Val Veeta" by Mel Ramos, is not without an awareness of formal structure, but it seems to be more of a literal statement than a visual one. What seems to be at stake, then, is the relative importance of form and content. By way of contrast, Warhol's "Elvis I and II" relies primarily on form, with content being of lesser importance. There are obvious visual similarities in the two; both contain figures that are placed centrally on the canvas, with no background, and both employ commercial techniques of paint application. Warhol's silk screen painting is a portrait of Elvis Presley, the figure repeated four times, two in color, two in a single hue. The Ramos is an oil painting of a nude posed on a box of cheese, the big difference between the wo

---

[65] Marks, 220.
[66] Marks.
[67] Marks.

being the label on the cheese box. There is subject matter in each, but the only comment in the Warhol is perhaps that Elvis is a fabricated hero. He used Elvis as an object upon which he can hang formal problems of visual relationships. Ramos, on the other hand, uses juxtaposition of words and images to make a sardonic comment on America. His slick painting style gives the nude an appearance of contrived sensuality. Her hair is a wig. There are no blemishes, no warts, no miles, no pimples, no scratches and no stretch marks. Neither wife nor mother, nor even lover, she is a commodity like Velveeta Cheese. The choice of brands is an obvious pun on the velvet smoothness of the girl, and a double pun on "cheesecake." The pun is re-emphasized by the word play in the title. And of course, Velveeta is a "process" rather than a natural cheese.

Collage

The collage technique has come a long way since Picasso and Braque first glued simulated textures on their still life arrangements, and today it remains a favorite technique. Since collage, as both media and a method of design, seems to be anti-linear, it is apropos to a "McLuhanesque" society.[68]

Two seemingly diverse but, perhaps, equally compelling reasons for the popularity of collage have been given by Warhol and Wesselmann:

> . . . One of the reasons I got started making collages was that I lacked involvement with the things I was painting; I didn't have enough interest in a rose to paint it. . . . I don't love roses or bottles or anything like that enough to want to sit down and paint them lovingly and patiently. [Warhol][69] . . . There's a

---

[68] Arranging cut-out of found images on a surface often defeats attempts at orderly arrangement according to preconceived plans or rules of perspective.
[69] Swenson, "What is Pop Art?" Russell and Gablik, p. 119.

shortage of collage material. So brushstrokes can occur, but they are often present as a collage element; . . .

>One thing I like about collage is that you can use anything, which gives you that kind of variety; it sets up reverberations in a picture from one kind of reality to another. [Wesselmann][70]

Warhol's stated reason for using collage may be a primary cause of its present popularity, expediency being very much a part of the whole aura of passivity and anti-aesthetics that seems to permeate the new art. Wesselmann, on the other hand, indicates the use of collage as both media and method, and cites the variety it affords.

One artist, Ray Johnson, has used collage so extensively and in so many ways that to people who are familiar with his work, the term *collage* has come to be almost synonymous with his name:

>Like information in newspapers, the images on a movie screen, the collages of Ray Johnson are continually changing and new ones come and take their place. Ultimately they take the form of mailings, surprises, presents which he distributes complexly according to the rules of a private game. It is a question of waiting, not for time to finish the work, but for time to indicate something one would not have expected to occur. . . . In the end they are more involved with intimacy than with public occasion. Art concerns a highly personal encounter with the spectator and what is said, after all, is quite second hand if said to someone else. "But I'll get you," he claims, "if it takes a day, a week, or a year. I'll cut you up. . . and if I can't do it myself I'll find someone who can."[71]

---

[70] Swenson, p. 120.
[71] Rusell an Gablik, p. 85.

Sitting comfortably outside the tradition of easel painting, Johnson has exhibited his work in such places as Grand Central Station, and the streets of New York. He stores his "moticos" in cardboard boxes, cuts them up, and mails them to friends.[72]

Johnson is also the founder of a "continuous 'postal Happening' in the form of the New York Correspondence School. . .,"[73] a unique, freewheeling form of Happening that is "performed" simultaneously in all parts of the world (primarily but not solely limited to the United States). The New York Correspondence School is made up of practically anyone and everyone, dependent on Johnson's personal discretion. The "events" are letters, clippings, drawings, bits of collages and photographs, which are mailed to various "members," who may alter them, forward them, return them, answer them or ignore them. The whole conglomeration is loosely held together by newsletters and meetings. The following is quoted in part from a New York Correspondence School newsletter:

> The New York Correspondence School has been asked to participate in the STILT MEETING to be held on the Central Park Mall (Fifth Avenue and 72nd street) on October 26th from 2-4 p.m. (cancelled if bad weather). You are asked to bring stilts, children on stilts, wear costumes, masks, bring packages, bundles, surprises and envelopes. There will be percussion music. Attach bells to stilts. Bring a post card.
>
> Will Steve Tyson, (address deleted) make the biggest pair of stilts in the world? Will Richard C, (address deleted) make a fake pair of stilts? . . . Will critic Lawrence Alloway (address deleted) find that stilts are objectless art? Will George Ashley, Hertz, (address deleted) invite Janis Joplin to wear her garters on a pair of stilts? Will Bill Berkson, (address deleted)

---

[72] "Moticos" is a self-invented name for Johnson's random arrangement of collages. Russell and Gablik, p. 17.
[73] Russell and Gablik.

be the best-dressed man on stilts? . . . Will May Wilson, Grandma of the Underground, wear a stilt stilt stilt necklace? . . . Will Ronald Gross, (address deleted) write a poem about stilts?[74]

---

[74] Russell and Gablik, p. 87.

Chapter IV

Conclusion

Certain generalizations have been made in this paper concerning the state of art in today's world. Furthermore, these generalizations have been made in view of certain historical-artistic developments, taking the Renaissance as a starting point and leading up to observable phenomena taking place in the contemporary world. Basically, the generalizations which have been made are: (1) The continuance of "new schools" of art is seemingly no longer a workable method of developing art. (2) For an increasing number of artists, the frame-pedestal aesthetic, which placed the artist as a special class of person and the artifact as a special class of object, is no longer a valid approach to art. Groups of artists whose numbers seem to the constantly increasing are replacing aesthetic concerns with new attitudes which are based on ethical posture.

    If the concepts put forth in this paper are valid, there is an implication that the very form by which they were expressed is in question, the more contemporary collage form being better suited to an exploration of today's art. Whereas an orderly arrangement according to outline form tends to isolate things which are actually related, the collage method allows for an infinite variety of relationships to become apparent.

Hopefully, the following collage of visual and verbal statements shall serve to summarize and amplify the text of this paper, as well as be entertaining to the reader.

". . . The major issues no longer hinge upon the creation of enduring masterpieces. . . . (Russell and Gablik, p. 12.)

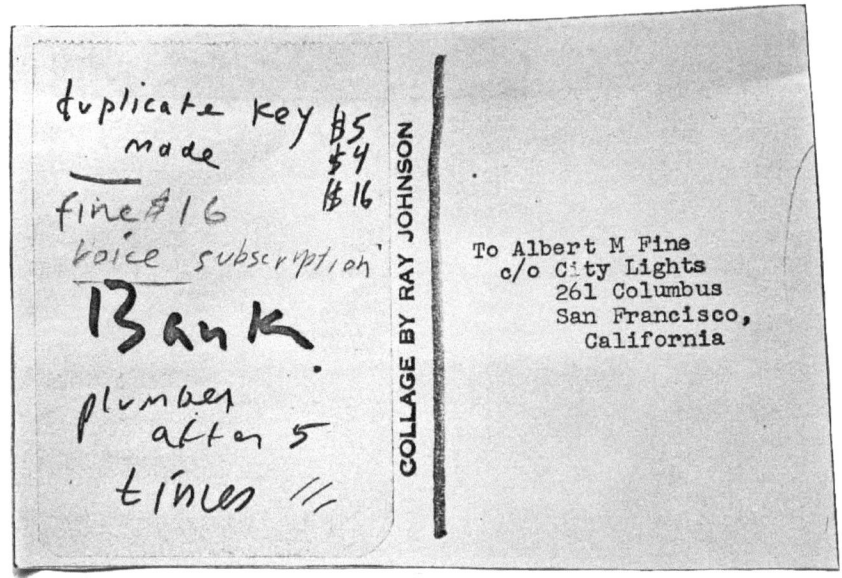

Figure 1. New York Correspondence School: collage by Ray Johnson

To design is to arrange with an awareness of every mark, word, sound, color, image, and shape, and its relationship or lack of relationship to every other mark-word-sound-color-image-shape, as well as to the field or format, and to do so with or without a preconceived plan or idea, to devise or not to devise a plan or idea while in the process, and to become aware of or feel some reaction to the completed design. The design must involve one thing—more or less. It may be actually executed or only conceived of or purposefully not conceived of. Also, sentences, both literary and judicial, should never end with prepositions.

Since art criticism is one of the few remaining branches of fiction that has not been exploited to the point of exhaustion, we may reasonably hope to see a broadening of its scope within the fairly near future. Its potential as a field of escapist or imaginative literature is enormous and, more fashionably, it may be thought of as an instrument of the struggle for the expansion of consciousness. No longer can any special prerogatives be awarded to the roles of artist, poet, critic, saint (if someone commissions a craftsman—by telephone—to put together a primary structure, is the resulting item art, poetry, criticism or a cipher for Nirvana?) In a spirit of splendid democracy everyone advances towards the common goal. The important thing, it seems, is to keep moving. (Finch, p. 134.).

We are just beginning to see the truth of dada—their time was behind them.

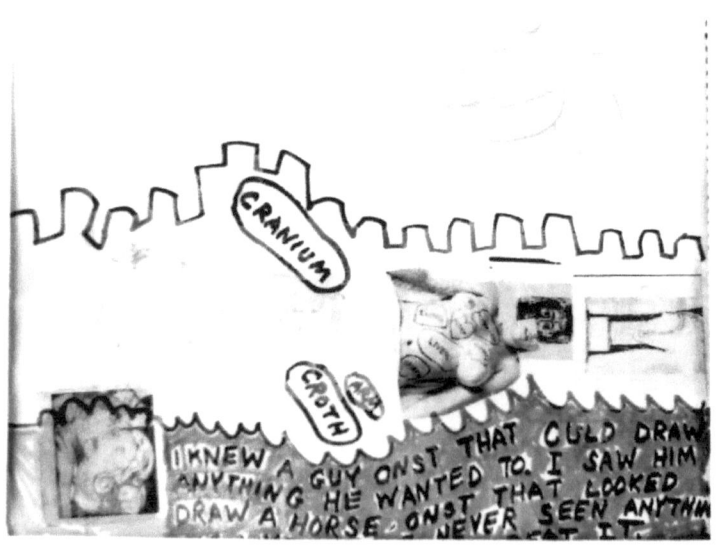

Figure 2. Collage by Alec Clayton

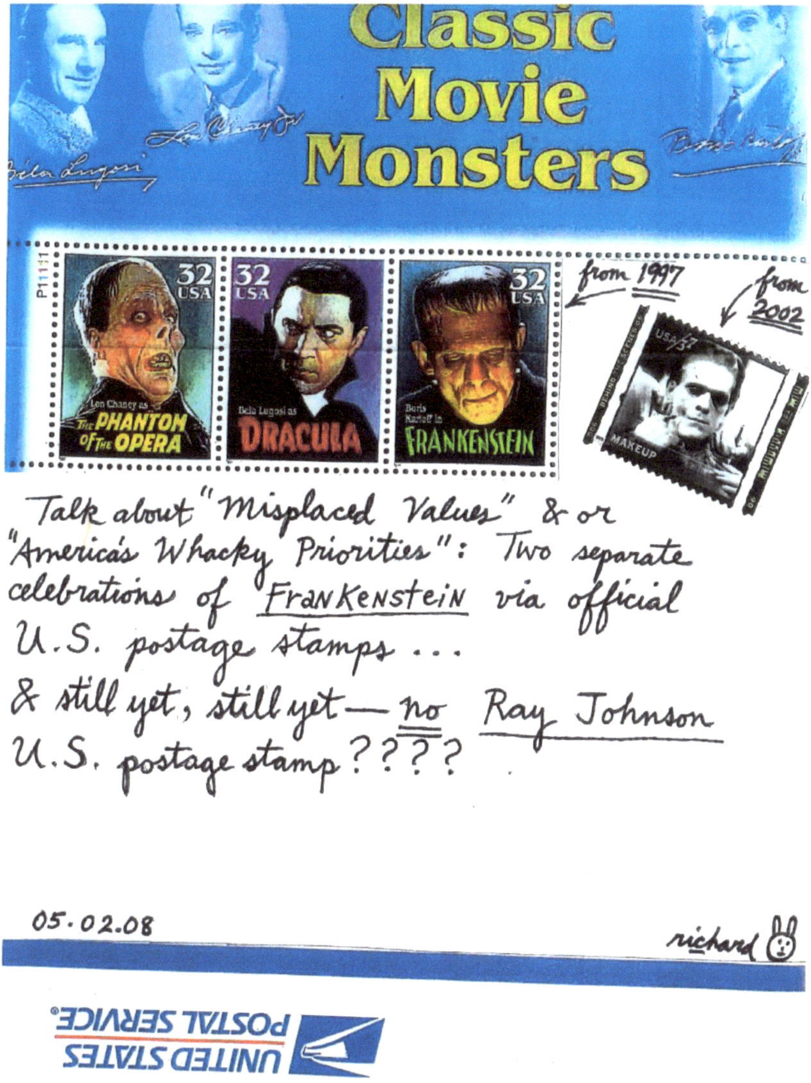

Talk about "Misplaced Values" & or "America's Whacky Priorities": Two separate celebrations of <u>FranKenstein</u> via official U.S. postage stamps ...
& still yet, still yet — <u>no</u> Ray Johnson U.S. postage stamp ????

05.02.08   richard

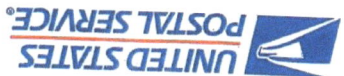

Figure 3. Mail art by Richard C

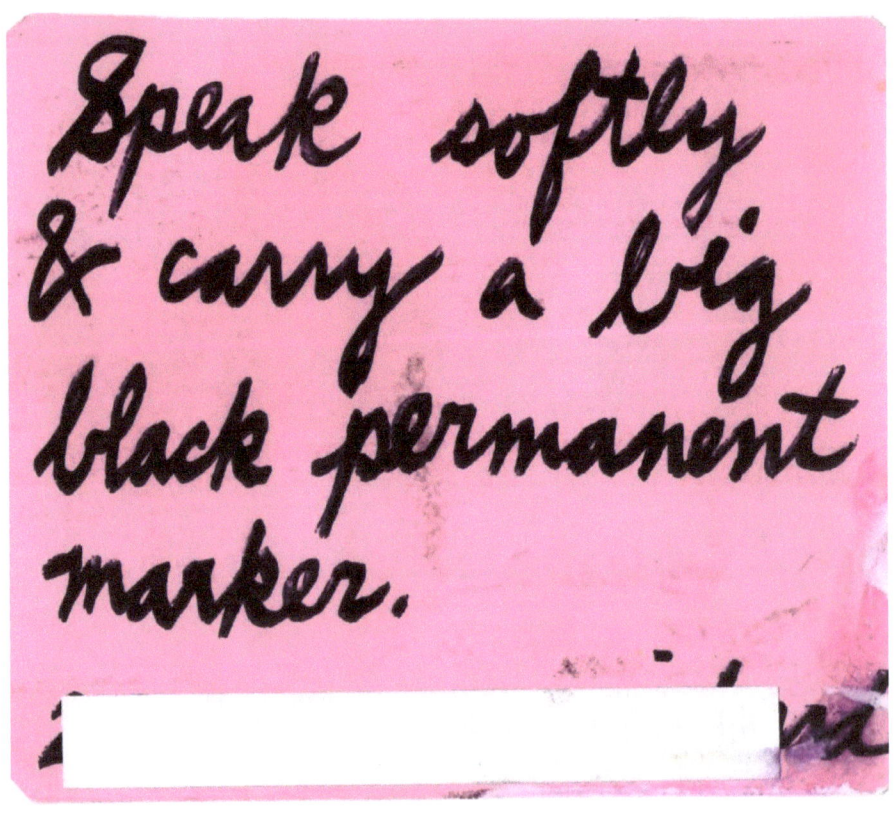

Figure 4. Mail art by Richard C

". . . Artistic activity is natural for man, and consequently should not be differentiated from any other form of activity." (Battcock, p. 182).

"One of the best ways to focus on youth humor is to point out what it is not. Jack E. Leonard it is not. . . . It is also not Bob Hope." (Marks, p. 218).

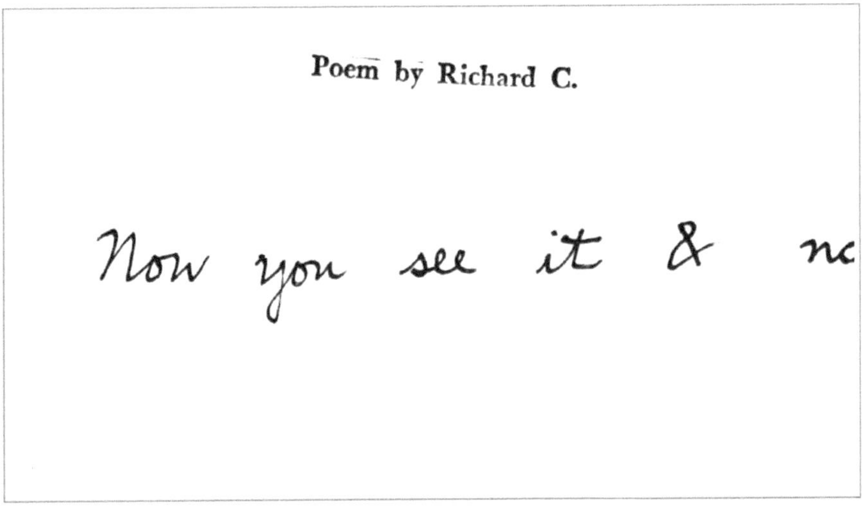

Poem by Richard C.

Now you see it & no

Figure 5. Mail art by Richard C

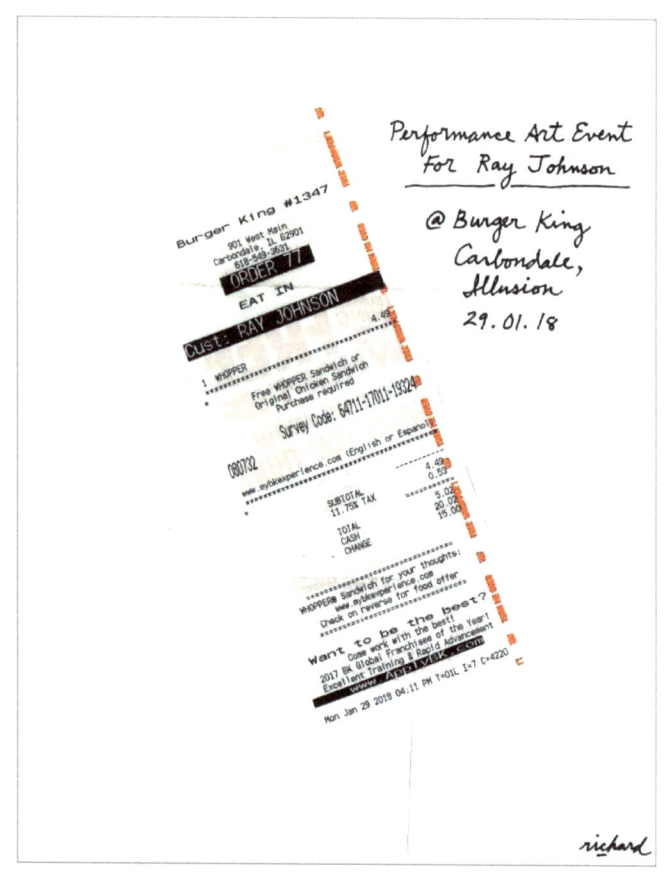

Figure 6. Mail art by Richard C

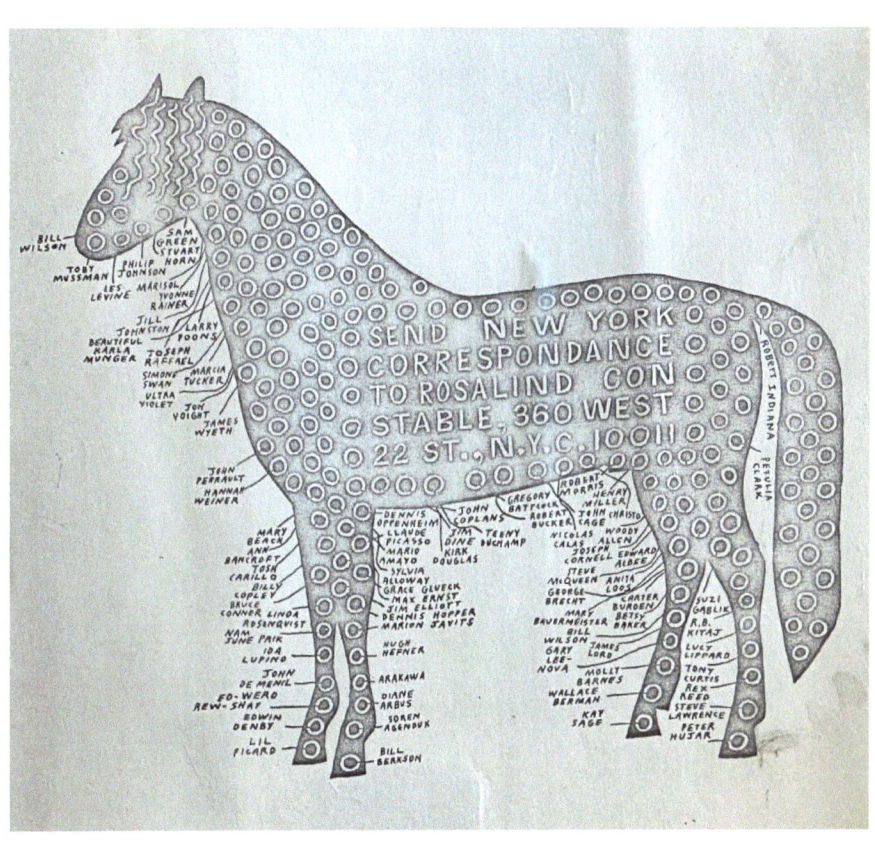

Figure 7. New York Correspondance School

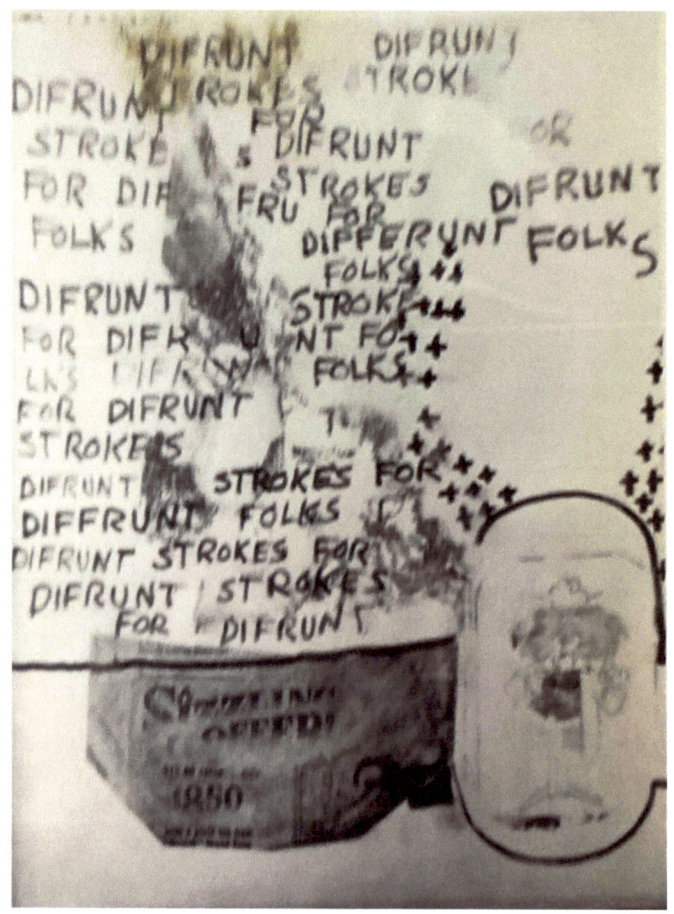

Figure 8. Collage by Alec Clayton

", , ,And who are you?" "I – I hardly know, sire, just at present. At least I know who I was when I got up this morning, but I think I must have changed several times since then." {From *Alice in Wonderland*, as quoted in McLuhan and Fiore).

Reproduction techniques can turn masterpieces into clichés overnight. (Rose, p. 219.).

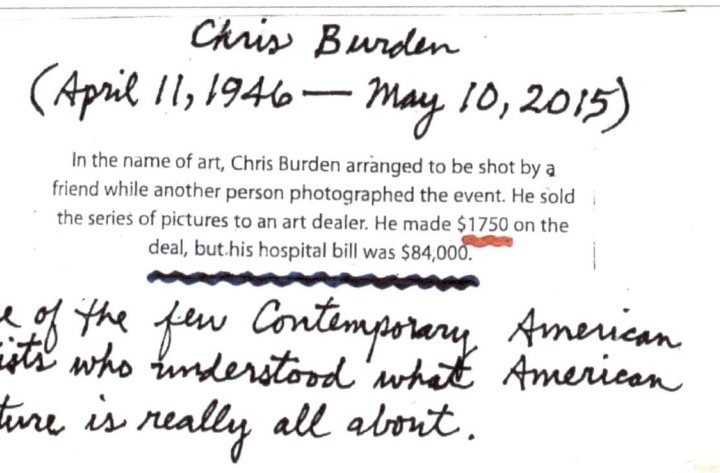

Figure 9. Mail art by Richard C

"One must be disinterested, accept that a sound is a sound and a man is a man, give up illusion about ideas of order, expressions of sentiment, and all the rest of our inherited clap-trap. (John Cage as quoted in McLuhan and Fiore).

"The highest purpose is to have no purpose at all." (Cage)

"Everyone is in the best seat." (Cage)

"History as she is harped.

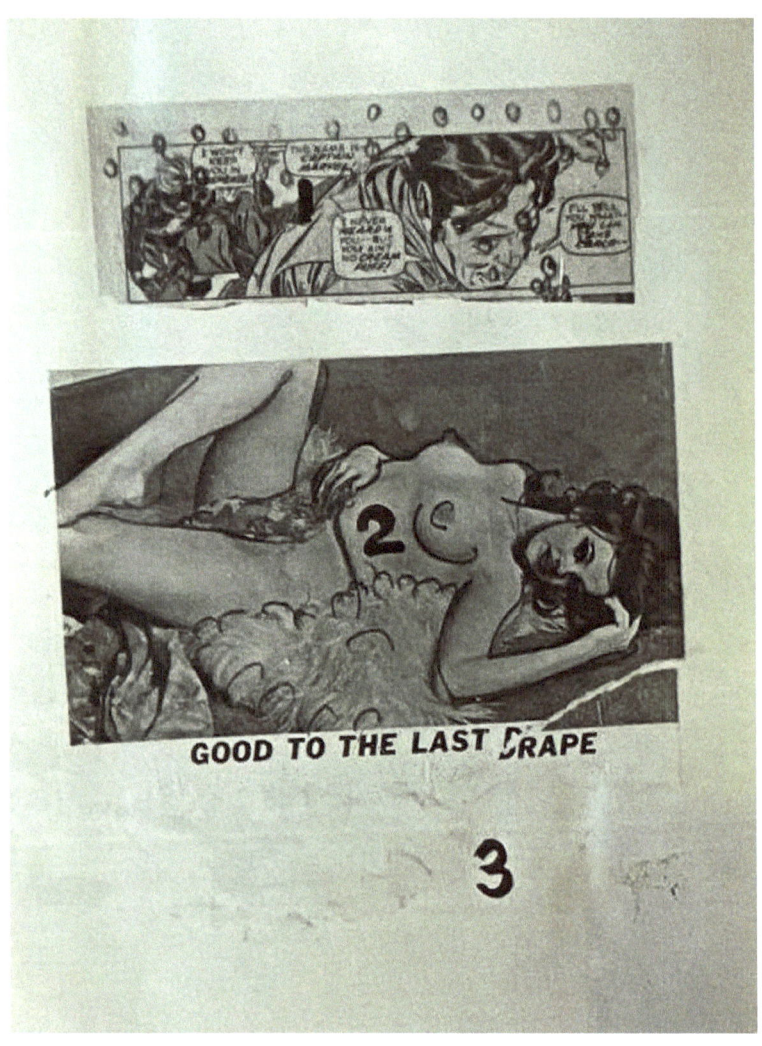

Figure 10. Collage by Alec Clayton

Rite words in rote order." (McLuhan and Fiore)

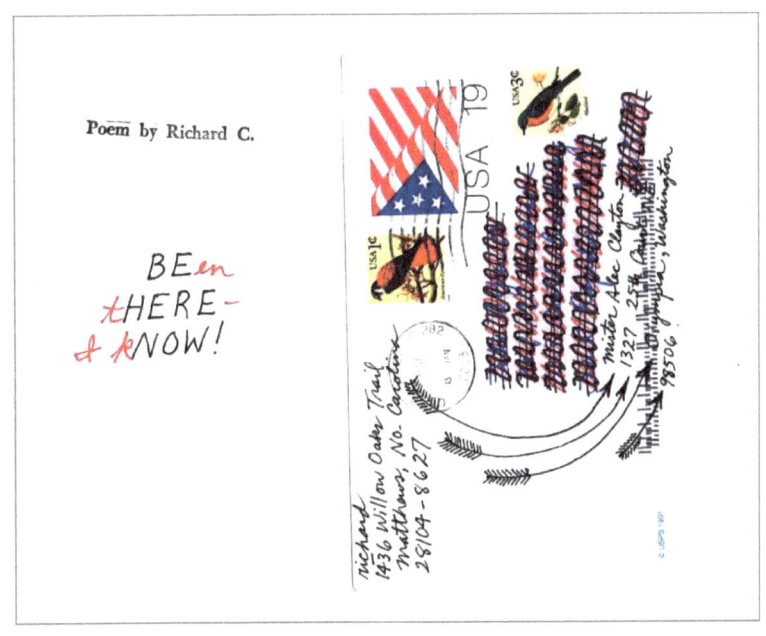

Figure 11. Mail art by Richard C

Afterword

Immediately before, during and after the time when I wrote this thesis, there was an exciting explosion of new art movements and new ideas afoot about what art could or should be. I was in my last years of undergraduate school and getting bored with the kind of art being produced in my college art department and shown in local museums and galleries, when all of a sudden I became aware of Pop Art, Environmental Art, Happenings, Color Field Painting, Hard Edge Abstraction, underground comics, a new form of Surrealism from a group of painters out of Chicago call the Hairy Who. In the parlance of the day, it blew my mind.

It was this cacophony of new and exciting art during my college years, coupled with meeting Richard C, who introduced me to the New York Correspondence School, that led me to the writing of this thesis. Richard forgot nothing. He would file away images, information, and the seemingly most trivial information until the perfect time arrived to use it in a collage or piece of mail art. For example, Richard and I shared a studio. I was painting large shaped canvases at the time, influenced by Frank Stella. I did small studies on cardboard for the larger paintings. After graduating, I left all the little studies behind. They had served their purpose. Richard saved those studies, or at least one of them, and many years later he cut pieces out of one of them and mailed them to Ray Johnson. Ray used them in a collage and sent it back to Richard. Richard rearranged the pieces into the shape of a tong and called it a "clay tong" and mailed it to me. I saved it. I treasure it. The "clay tong" is a collage by Richard C., Ray Johnson, and me. It epitomizes for me what collage as a method of design is all about, and what the New York Correspondence School is all about—connections. It also, to me, coming as such a surprise years after I did those little studies, epitomizes what Ray Johnson meant when he said, "But I'll get you, if it takes a day, a week, or a year. I'll cut you up . . . and if I can't do it myself I'll find someone who can."

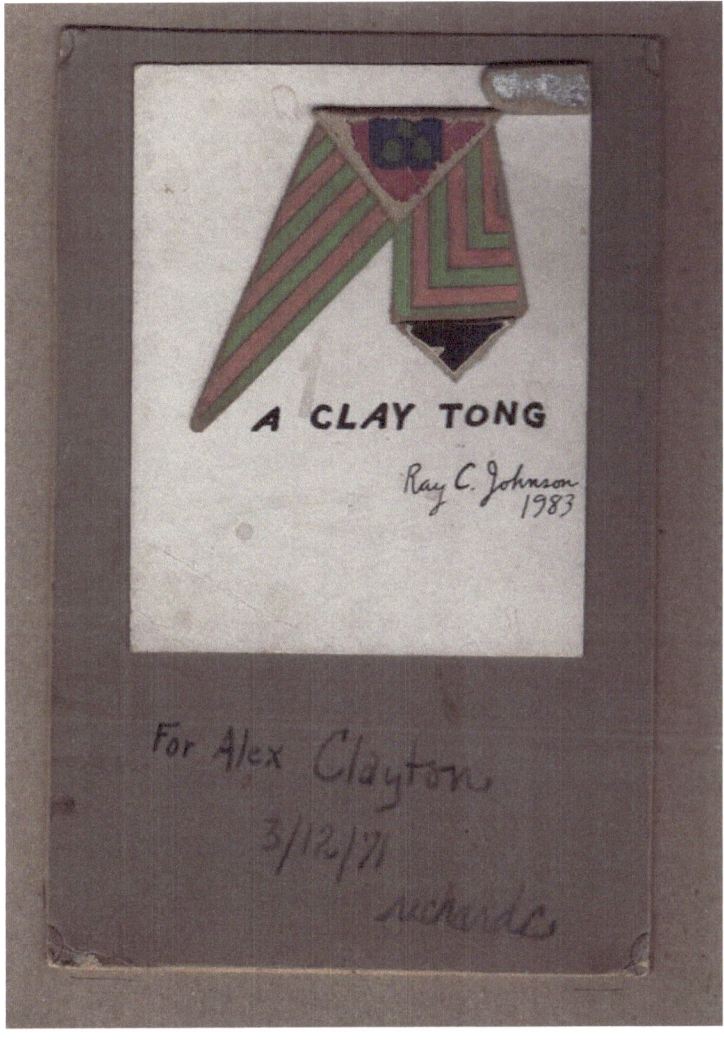

Figure 12. Collage by Ray Johnson, Richard C, and Alec Clayton

Since my thesis was written, the explosion of new art has perhaps slowed down but has not ceased. Such things as Graffiti Art, Earth Art (sculptural forms in nature made from rocks, soil, water and not intended to last by such artists as Andy Goldsworthy, Robert Smithson and Richard Long), such things as Christo and Jeanne Claude's "Running Fence" and wrapped islands and buildings. New forms of performance and installation art remain a vital part of the world of art.

A Londoner, Jason deCaires Taylor, creates underwater installations called underwater museums or sculpture parks that are intended to become integral parts of the underwater eco systems.

Beginning in 1970, the year I wrote this thesis, Ed McGowin legally changed his name twelve times, creating a new identity under each name and creating works of art under each. As Renato Denese then wrote (quoted from McGowin's website: http://www.edmcgowin.com/namechange_t1.html) "At the heart of McGowin's thinking, however, is the idea of change. An artist's will to change, he believes, has been denied him throughout history by the repressive demand that his work develop in a sequentially logical, linear progression. A condition of art history has been that the artist should present us with a consistent body of work."

In 1972, McGowin exhibited works from all twelve artists at the Baltimore Museum of Art, and he has continued to make art under the different names since.

Pacific Northwest environmental artist Barbara de Pirro creates what art writer Lisa Kinoshita calls "a sometimes harrowing vision both of what nature is, and what it is being subsumed by: ecological catastrophe." She builds forms out of discarded plastic bags and bottles and crochets limbs and vines out of discarded commercial materials and sites them in natural settings as well as in buildings. Kinoshita describes a de Pirro installation on Camano Island in Washington as "eerie, beautiful and slightly repulsive. Like a parasitic plant, the heavy-laden vines clung to the evergreen's thick trunk, never to decompose."

Living, breathing, moving sculptures dot the desert landscape at the annual Burning Man festival in Nevada. Artist Teri Bevelacqua created for Burning Man a billboard made up of ten twenty-four-inch-square encaustic paintings on moveable panels that is lighted for nighttime viewing. Viewers can rearrange the panels to their liking. Bevelacqua's billboard is pictured on the cover of this book.

In 1970, I saw this thesis as a manifesto. I believed that what I thought of as the new art would replace everything that came before. I thought that making objects to be admired for their beauty was no longer a viable activity. As such, I refused to do a graduate exhibit, which was required for graduation. I had to defend that decision before a faculty panel—a trial as it were—and I successfully used this thesis as my defense. Since then, in a half century as a painter and art critic, some of my ideas have changed, some perhaps softened a little. I realized long ago that new art forms did not have to replace the old but could live alongside them.

Post-Postmodern Postscript

One final addendum. I did not mention the critic Clement Greenberg in my thesis. That was a major oversight. Greenberg was perhaps the most influential art critic of the twentieth century. Derisively called Pope Clement by some artists, a review by Greenberg could make or break an artist.

Greenberg seldom if ever wrote about sculpture or performance art or any art form other than painting. To him, painting was the be-all and end-all of art; and a painting according to him was an arrangement of shapes and colors on a flat surface, nothing more and nothing less. Recognizable subject matter had to go, as did any illusion of depth. It was all about form, not content.

In his early years he championed Abstract Expressionism and Willem de Kooning in particular. Later in his career he championed Color Field Painting and Jules Olitski in particular. As late as 1990, long after Greenberg had pronounced Color Field Painting the rightful heir to Abstract Expressionism, he said Olitski was "the best painter alive." By then, Greenberg's ideas about art had become so reductive and restrictive there was hardly anything left a painter could do.

At the time I wrote this thesis, Greenberg's writings were barely a blip on my radar. Ironically, in light of the ideas I expressed in my thesis, beginning in about 1980 I started a revised career as a painter and critic, and Greenbergian formalism dominated both my paintings and my art writing. It was not that I had given up my ideas of art as an ethical rather than an aesthetic pursuit (see page 7); it was simply that I loved playing with colors and shapes and textures on a flat surface, and I loved looking at paintings that gave dominance to form over content. That might seem retrograde in light of the ideas expressed in my thesis, but I see it now as simply one of many viable approaches to artmaking. As John Cage said, "The situation must be yes-and-no not either-or. . . . Everything we do is Music."

Bibliography

Battock, Gregory (ed.). *The New Art*. New York: E.P. Dutton and Co., Inc., 1966.

Carroll, Paul. "What's a Warhol?" *Playboy*, September 1969, p. 133-140 and 278-282.

Finch, Christopher. *Pop Art: Object and Image*. New York: E.P. Dutton and Co., Inc., 1968.

Ghiselin, Brewster (ed.). *The Creative Process*. New York: Mentor, 1952.

Hayes, Harold T.P. (ed.). "Work in Progress," *Esquire*, December 1969. P. 212.

Hunter, Sam. *Modern American Painting and Sculpture*. New York: Dell publishing Co., Inc., 1959.

Jean, Marcel. The History of Surrealist Painting. Taylor, Simon Watson (trans.). New York: Dell publishing Co., Inc., 1960.

Kaprow, Allan. *Assemblage, Environments and Happenings*. New York: Harry N. Abrams, Inc., 1966.

Kaprow, Allan. "The Legacy of Jackson Pollock," Art News, October 1958. Pp. 24, ff.

Marks, J. "The New Humor," Esquire, December 1969. Pp. 218-220 and 329-330.

McLuhan, Marshall and Fiore, Quintin. The Medium is the Message. New York: Bantam Books, Inc., 1967.

Rose, Barbara. *American Art Since 1900*. New York: Freerick A. Praeger, 1969.

Russell, John and Gabli, Suzi. *Pop Art Redefined*. New York: Freerick A. Praeger, 1969.

Stearn, Gerald E., McLuhan: Hot and Cool. New York: Signet. 1969.

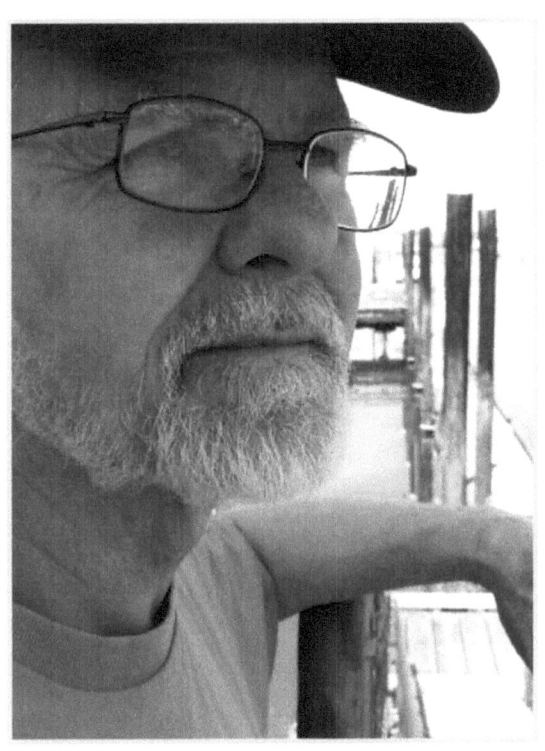

About Alec Clayton

Alec Clayton is a novelist, newspaper columnist, painter, art critic, and co-founder with his wife, Gabi Clayton, of Mud Flat Press. He graduated with a Master of Art in Drawing and Painting from East Tennessee State University in 1970. His paintings have been shown in galleries throughout some of the United States. He has written art criticism for The Weekly Volcano (Tacoma, Washington), Oly Arts (Olympia, Washington), Art Access (Seattle, Washington). Mississippi Arts & Letters (Hattiesburg, Mississippi) and other publications. He lives and works in Olympia, Washington.

http://alecclayton.com
http://mudflatpress.com

www.ingramcontent.com/pod-product-compliance
Lightning Source LLC
Chambersburg PA
CBHW040324220526
45473CB00009B/2564